WHY DIDN'T Somebody TELL ME?

WHY DIDN'T *Somebody* TELL ME?

Written by
Dr. Francesica Kelley

Illustrated by
Ollie Ruth Humphrey

Copyright

Printed in the United States of America

First Printing, 2017

Edited by Ingrid Zacharias

Cover Art by Tanner Gary

Illustrated by Ollie Ruth Humphrey

ISBN-13: 978-0-9909919-7-7

ISBN10: 0990991970

Scriptures are taken from or based on the King James Version of the Bible.

The Butterfly Typeface Publishing
PO BOX 56193
Little Rock Arkansas 72215

Dedication

I dedicate this book to my mother, Mary Florine Swanigan,
who gave her life to her eight children.
She was a phenomenal mother who loved God and life itself.
She taught us to love God and each other by her unselfish examples.
To my Father, Burel Smith and Grandparents, Elbert and Lois Swanigan
who taught me respect, integrity and discipline.
I learned at an early age the importance of good manners,
responsibility and hard work.
I hope that I have lived my life in such a way that it will be a legacy
of Faith and Hope
for my children, grandchildren and great grandchildren.

"Suffer the little children
and forbid them not
for of such is the kingdom of heaven."

Revelations 7:14b

Foreword

I have often said that God really loves me because He gave me the best mother in the world. Not because she spoiled me, but because she demanded that I acquire knowledge, even if it meant having conversations with me that other parents weren't having with their children.

I am so grateful for conversations I had with my mother about love, hate, law, fairness, kindness, sex, tithing, positivity, work ethic, networking, spirituality, religion, academic excellence, personal growth, hygiene, boyfriends, being a wife, financial literacy, being a mother....I could go on and on and on.

"Why Didn't Somebody Tell Me" promises to open eyes and hearts to the very basic and central necessary conversations that have gone lacking in modern child-rearing. Fran (my Mother), as always, gives a candid and "in-your-face" perspective on various topics which, if discussed early and properly, will undeniably create meaningful discussions among parents and children, including those who are acting in a guardian or parental role. I cannot wait to hear the conversations that will be birthed from this book!

~LaTonya L. Austin

Foreword

As a Foster Parent, I am often taken aback at the many children who have come into my home, who have *never been taught*. They've never been taught to say thank you, to brush their teeth, to bathe daily, to love, to live, to simply be…

This book by Dr. Fran Kelley is such a necessary guide to the things we so often take for granted. "Why Didn't Somebody Tell Me" promises to be a best seller.

~LaFrancis Phifer

Acknowledgments

This book is for the millions of boys and girls. Many may have suffered some form of abuse or disability and may need special attention. They may just need a few extra minutes at bedtime or a few extra moments of reading time during the day. Whatever your situation, I have spent time meditating over these scriptures and I know that whatever your need is if you have faith, you will be richly blessed by sharing them with that special child in your life. Teach them to observe all things because "LIFE" has no boundaries. When they leave your presence they may be face with any situation. They need to know how you would want them to respond. For many years as a child I was bullied, and mistreated because I was different. I feel I allowed much of that time to be stolen from me because of my own insecurities.

I spent years of what if, because I listened to the negative words of other children calling me names like you're black, your hair is short, you're too tall, and your eyes are big and so on. I didn't know how to turn those negative words into positive ones. I want to teach young people who may feel that they don't measure up to feel good within their own skin. I hope they will learn to concentrate on their future, envision new projects, and dream of a life of success. In order to do that we must make a conscious effort little by little, step by step, day by day to see a gradual improvement. At some point in our lives we are or have all been ashamed or embarrassed by something that we've done.   We try to do better and not make that same mistake again.

The apostle Paul struggled, and stated, "I do not understand what I do; for what I want to do I do not do, but what I hate I do" (Romans NIV). In spite of our short comings, we must learn to be patient with ourselves and those who are mean to us. My suggestion is not from a perfection Of my own, I realize that it is the actions that we take which will make a difference in others' lives and especially our own.

So let's all take one step each day toward spreading God's Love to others and allow our thoughts and actions to be more in line with His. As Parents take time to show love to your child. Read to them regularly, and pray with them at bedtime. Encourage them daily to be all they want to be with what they have and create resources for what they don't have.

Life is Just a Minute…

I have only just a minute,
Only sixty seconds in it.
Forced upon me, can't refuse it.
Didn't seek it, didn't choose it.
But it's up to me to use it.
I must suffer if I lose it.
Give account if I abuse it.
Just 1 tiny little minute,
But eternity is in it.

Anonymous

I'd like to think that I have used my minutes well;
to the fullest of my ability.
I realize that I have made mistakes, and that I am going to make more.
However, I am doing my best to correct those by the positive examples
I try to leave in my life today. One might argue that our predestined course
may not actually be mistakes,
but rather the journey that God intended for us to take.
Whatever **your** course,
I trust that it is a positive productive perseverance in the things of God,
full of peace and gratitude.
~Dr. Fran Kelley

God is great.
God is good,
and we thank Him for our food.
By His hand, we all are fed;
thank you Lord,
for our daily bread.

~unknown

Why didn't Somebody tell me that there would be many things
that I would need to learn in order to be a successful person
to my family and community?
Don't get me wrong
I had the best of parents and grandparents who nurtured me well.
But still there were so many things that l missed.
I look at our young people today,
and so many are being raised by teenagers themselves.
They don't have the wisdom or the want-to, in most cases,
of how to be good parents.
Parental education and neglect has smothered this generation.
Many children start out in the first grade, and can't spell their name,
can't count 10, don't know any of their colors
or the basics such as **singing** their ABC's.
Let's see how much you know...

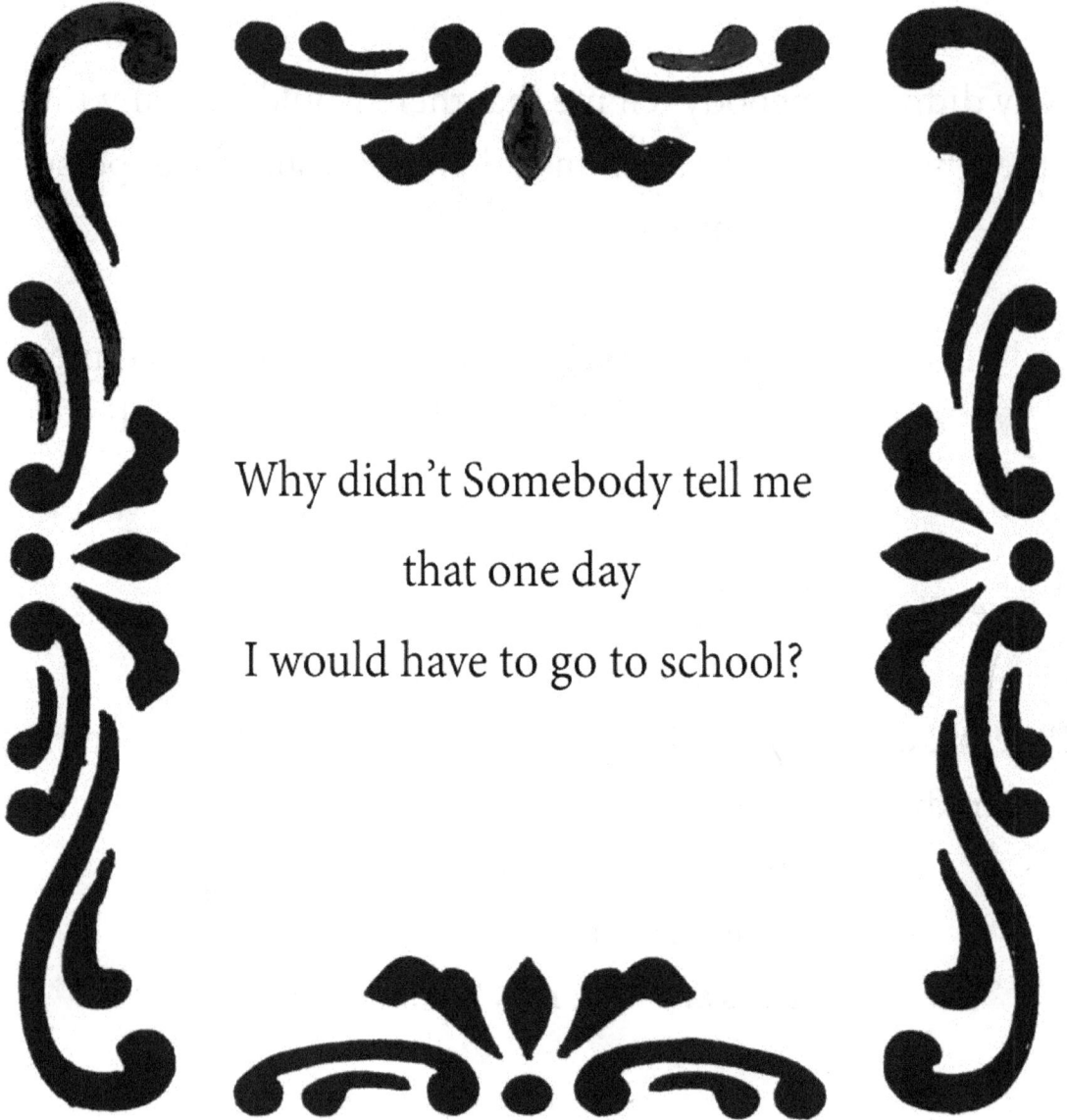

Why didn't Somebody tell me

that one day

I would have to go to school?

"Getting a good education is the most important tool to help you become successful."

Why didn't Somebody teach me

how to read?

"A mind is a terrible thing to under utilize."

Why didn't Somebody teach me

how to sit like a young lady?

"Poise and grace are the hallmarks of being a lady."

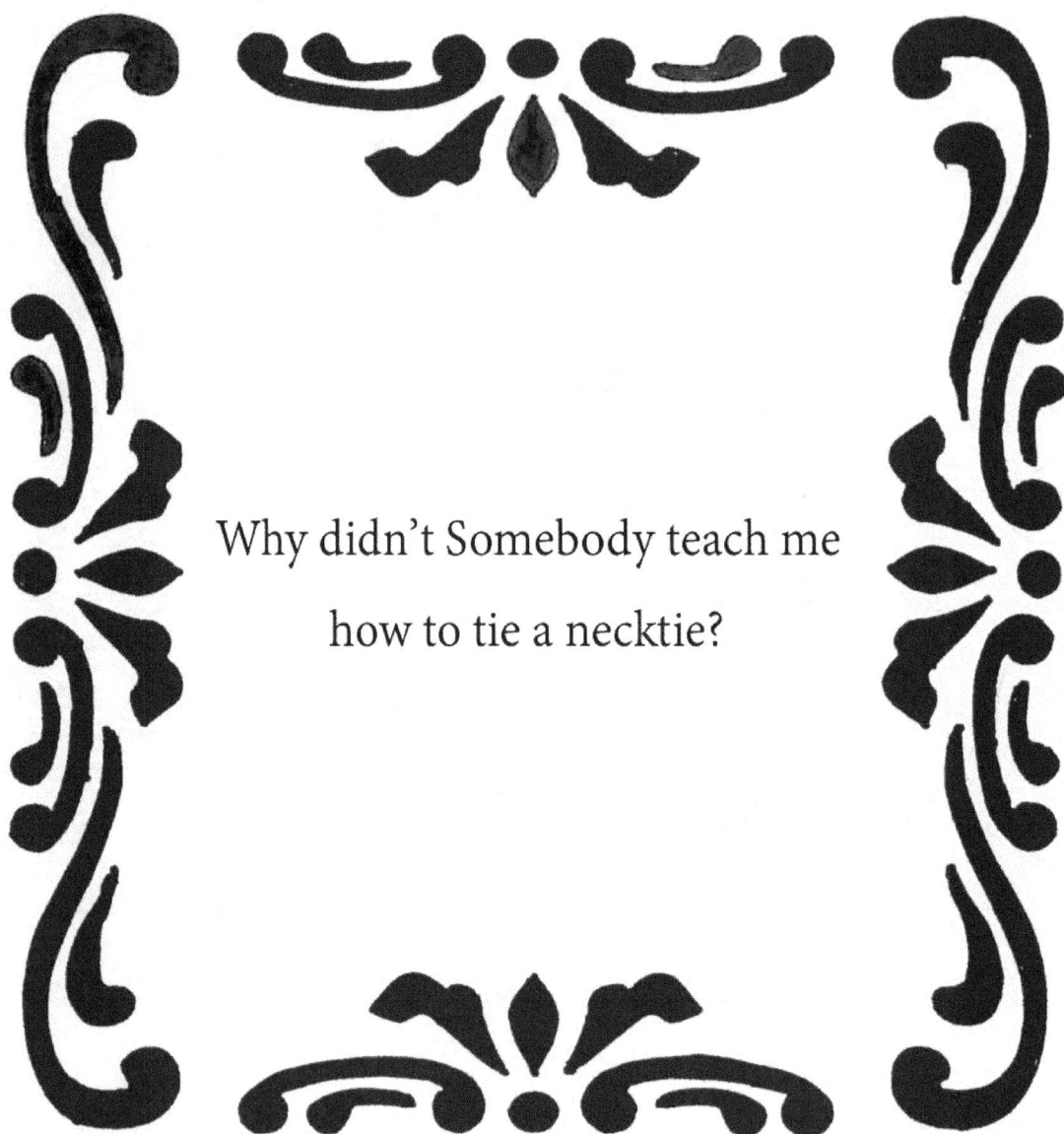

Why didn't Somebody teach me

how to tie a necktie?

"All young men should be able to tie a tie.

If you never learn, it doesn't mean that you aren't a man,

it just means that it will be a little complicated for you getting dressed as an adult."

Why didn't Somebody teach me

how to wash my face?

"Taking care of your skin is very important."

Why didn't Somebody teach me

how to comb my hair?

"Grooming is part of who you are."

Why didn't Somebody teach me

how to clean my room?

"Cleanliness is the next thing to Godliness."

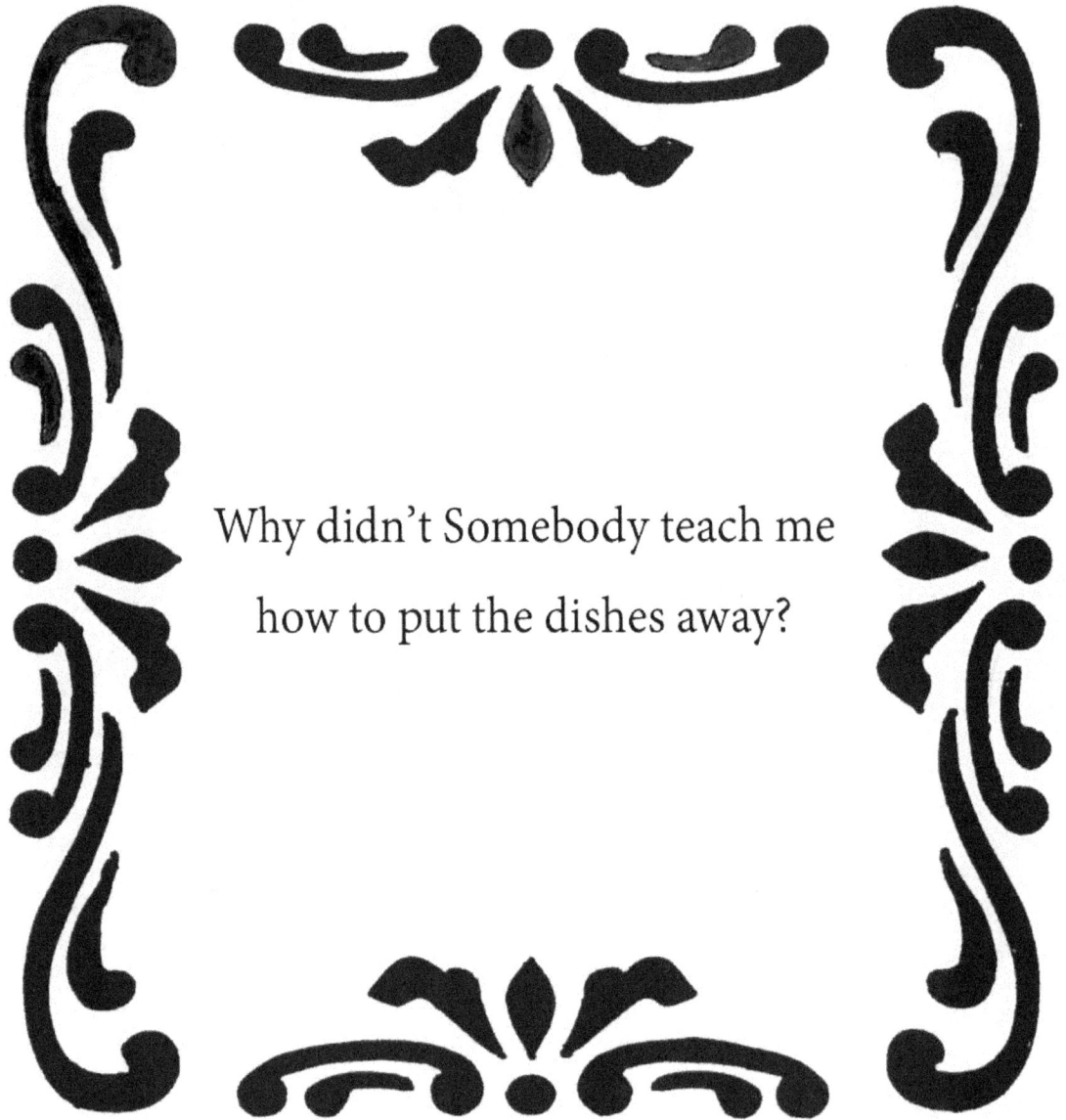

Why didn't Somebody teach me

how to put the dishes away?

"Learning how to be responsible and contribute to the household builds character."

Why didn't Somebody teach me

how to say grace?

"Thanking God is always in order."

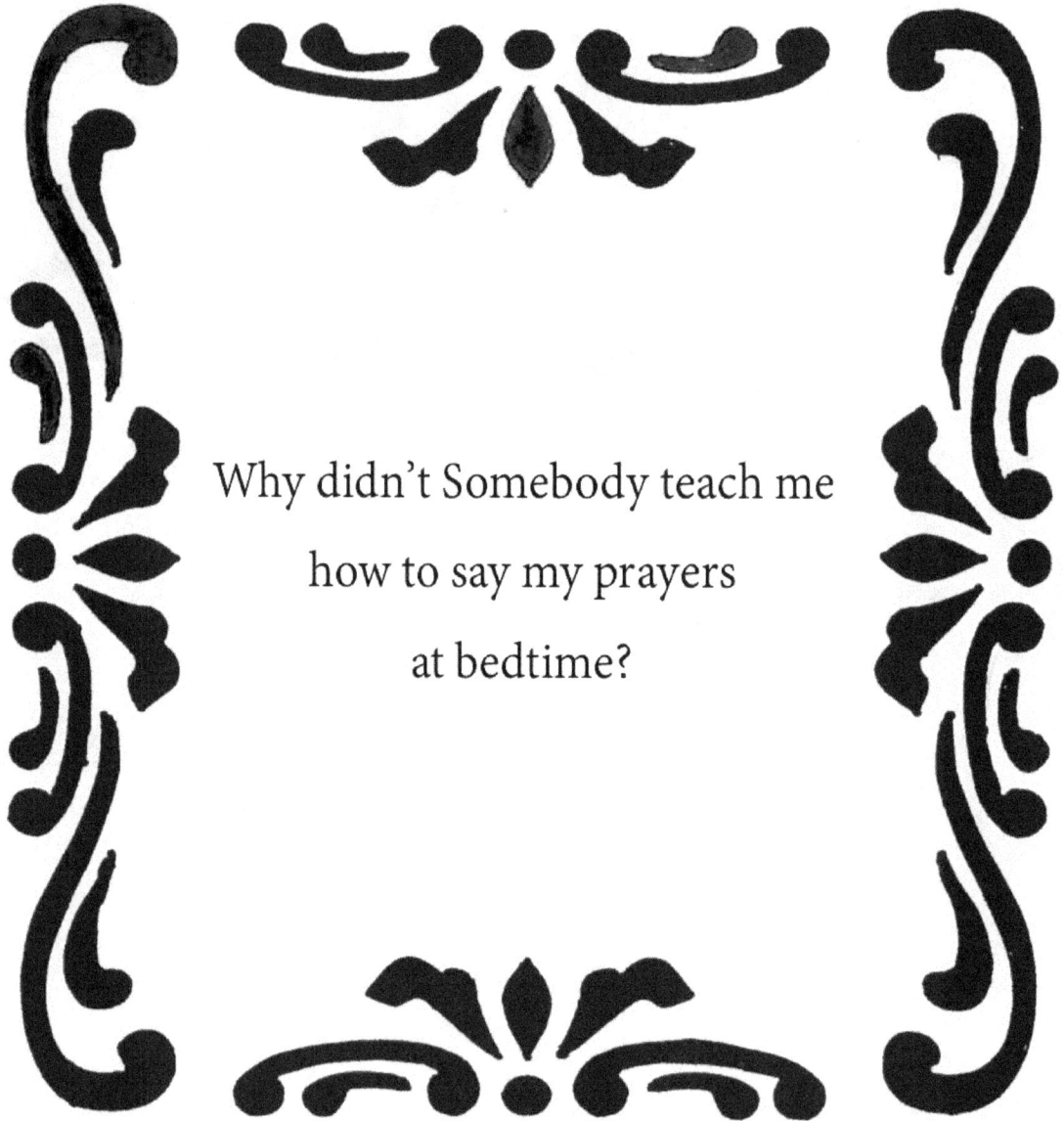

Why didn't Somebody teach me

how to say my prayers

at bedtime?

"Learning to pray will teach you many things,
especially how to be humble and grateful."

Why didn't Somebody teach me

how to cross the street safely?

"Learning to be safe is always important."

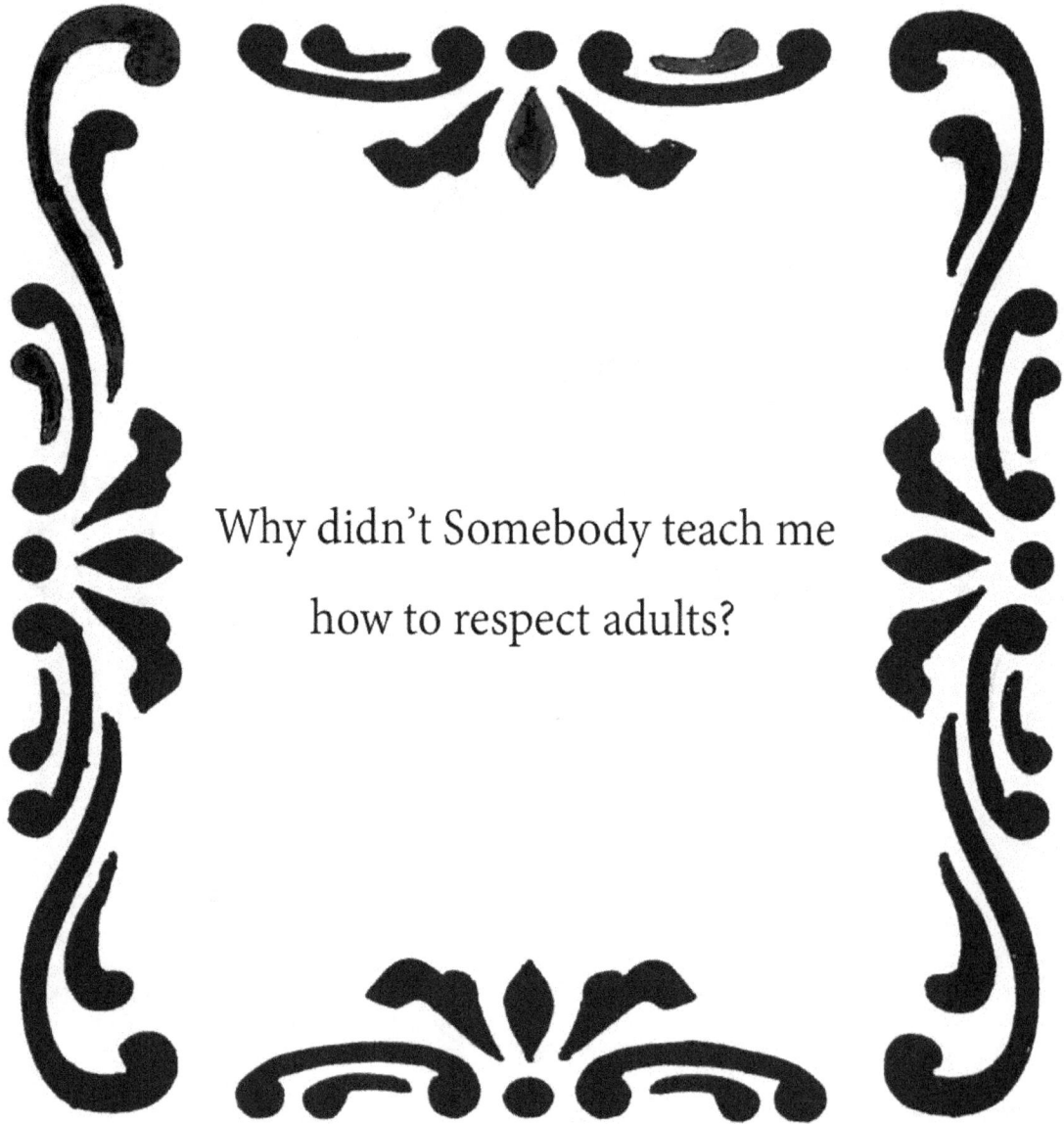

Why didn't Somebody teach me

how to respect adults?

"Learning to respect our parents and other adults is the prime virtue on which all other virtues are built."

Why didn't Somebody teach me

how to take a bath?

"Do you not know that you are God's temple and that God's spirit dwells in you?"

Why didn't Somebody teach me

how to order from a menu?

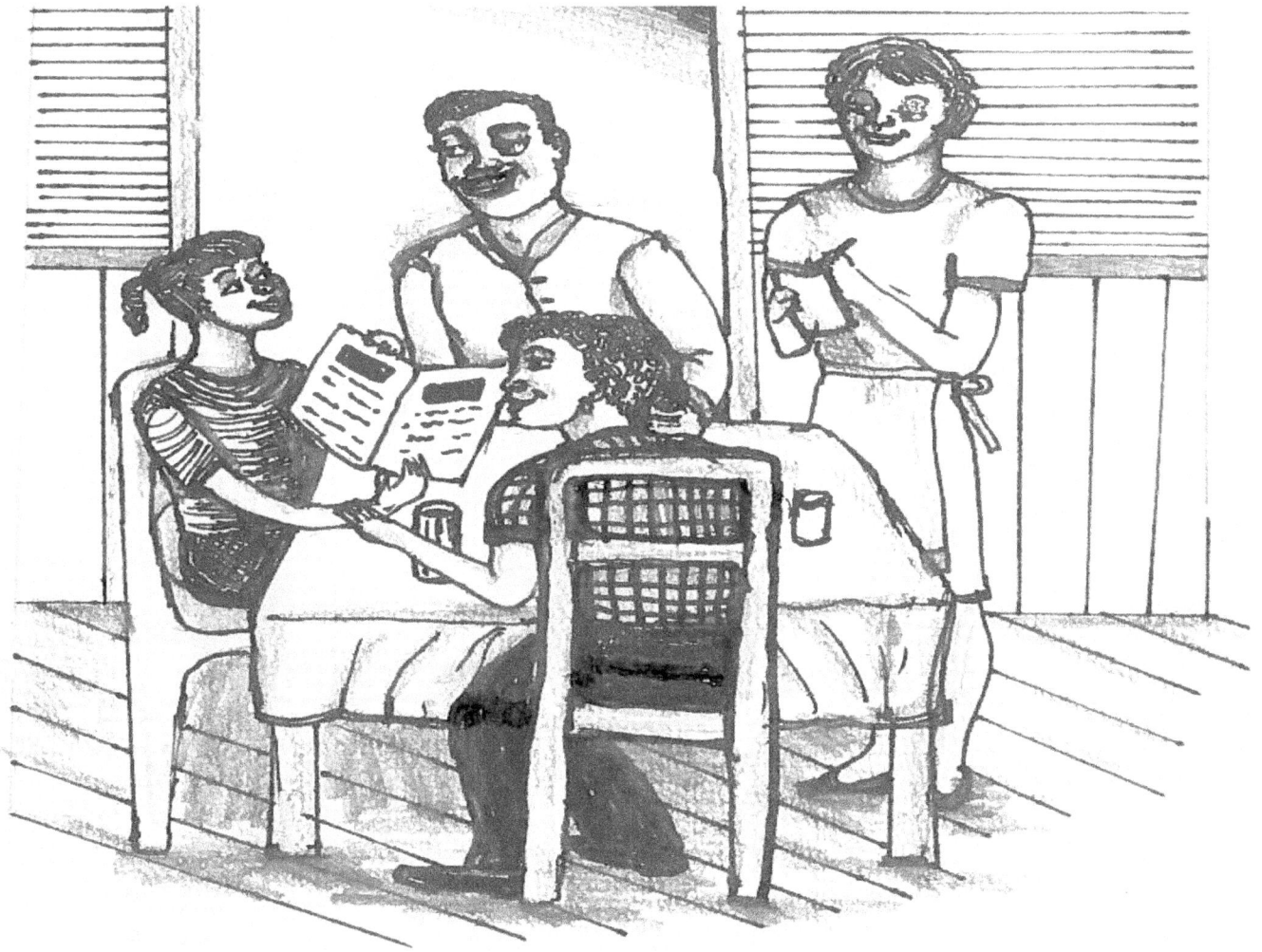

"It's important for you to learn how to present yourself in public."

Why didn't Somebody teach me

how to brush my teeth?

"A bad smelling breath is offensive."

Why didn't Somebody teach me

how to write my name?

"What's in a name? Everything! It's who you are and how you express yourself. Most of all, how you get paid. You must be able to sign your name on your check."

Why didn't Somebody teach me

how to say my ABCs?

"This is the basics of learning. This is your road map to learning how to read."

Why didn't Somebody teach me

how to tie my shoes?

"You need to know how to be prepared to move forward in life."

Why didn't Somebody teach me

how to put on my clothes?

"I must learn to dress for success inside and out."

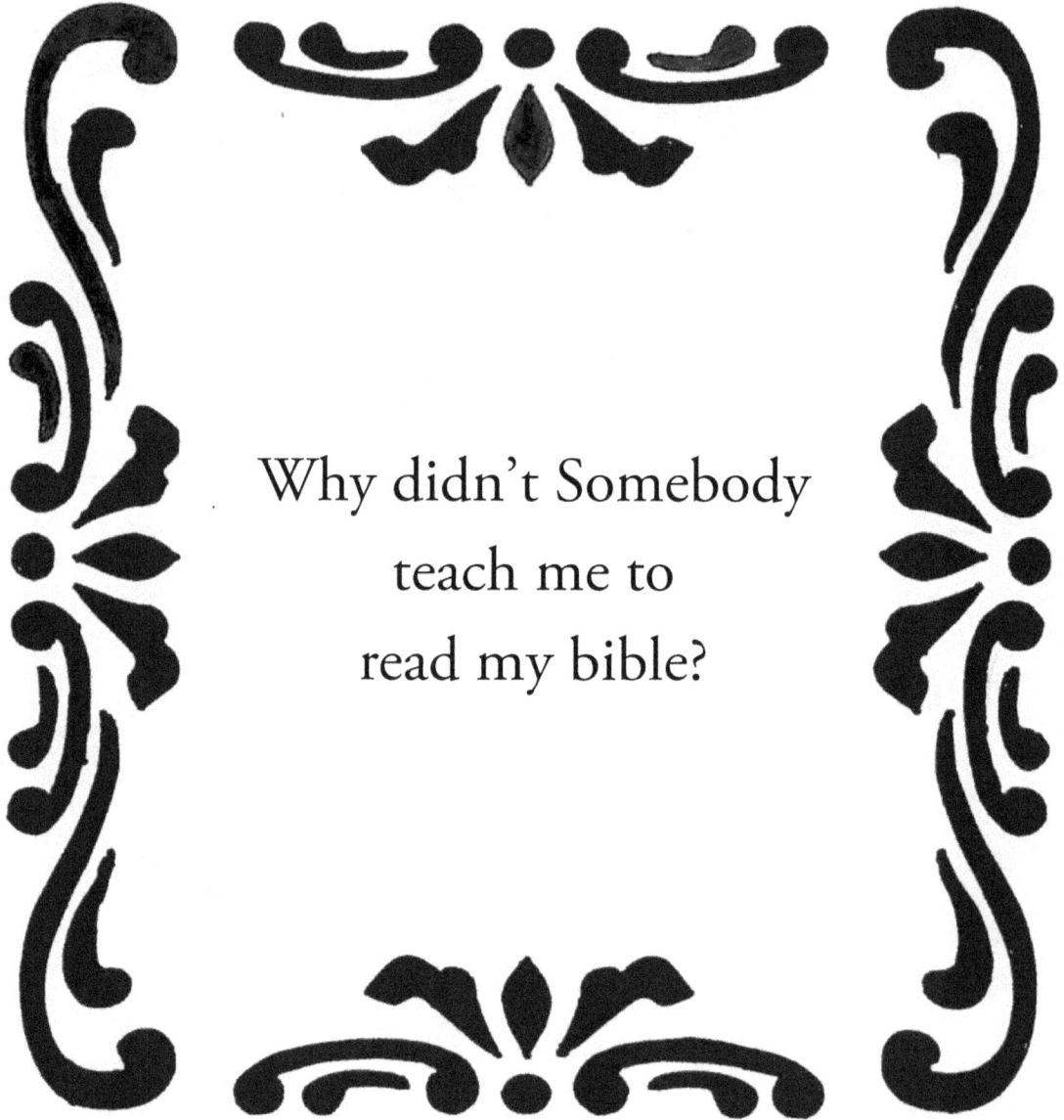

Why didn't Somebody
teach me to
read my bible?

"When you learn scriptures as a young person,
it builds a foundation for a strong spiritual life."

Reading and understanding what you read is the gateway to a fulfilled life. Reading and understanding scripture is the foundation for your Spiritual road map. You need to be able to draw and understand your own road map, so that you can draw your own conclusions and not be brainwashed or misled by someone else's views.

I will guide
thee with mine
eye.
-Psalm 32:8b

His compassions fail not. They are new every morning.

-Lamentations 3:22b

Trust in the Lord with all thine heart; and lean not unto thine own understanding.

-Proverbs 3:5

The Lord shall open unto thee his good treasure.

-Deuteronomy 28:12a

The Lord
loveth the
righteous.
-**Psalm 146:8**

Happy is the man that findeth wisdom, and the man that getteth understanding.

-Proverbs 3:13

He that keepth thee shall not slumber.

-Psalms 121:3b

Wisdom is the principal thing; therefore get wisdom: and with all thy getting get understanding.

-**Proverbs** 4:7

Therefore
being justified
by faith, we
have peace
with God.

-Romans 5:1

THEREFORE BEING JUSTIFIED BY FAITH, WE HAVE PEACE WITH GOD

ROMANS 5:1

I can do all
things through
Christ which
strengtheneth
me.
**-Philippians
4:13**

For I give you good doctrine, forsake not my law.

-**Proverbs 4:2**

Thou shalt call,
and I will
answer thee.

-Job 14:15a

He … giveth grace unto the humble.

-James 4:6c

Children obey your parents in the Lord: for this is right.

-**Ephesians 6:1**

Forasmuch as
ye know that
your labor is
not in vain in
the Lord.
**-I Corinthians
15:58b**

Honor thy
father and
mother which
is the first
commandment
with promise.
-Ephesians 6:2

O taste and see that the Lord is good: blessed is the man that trusteth in him.

-**Psalms 34:8**

O give thanks
unto the Lord
for he is good
and his mercy
endureth
forever.

-Psalm 106:1b

For with God
nothing shall
be impossible.
-Luke 1:37

No weapon
that is formed
against thee
shall prosper.
-Isaiah 54:17a

In the time of trouble he shall hide me in his pavilion.

-**Psalm 27:5a**

Make a joyful
noise unto the
Lord, all ye
lands.

-Psalm 100:1

There shall be
no evil befall
thee.
-Psalm 91:10a

The Lord is my
light and my
salvation,
whom shall I
fear? The Lord
is the strength
of my life; of
whom shall I
be afraid.

-Psalm 27:1

God is with thee in all that thou doest.

-Genesis 21:22b

Thou has been faithful over a few things, I will make tee ruler over many things.

-Matthew 25:23b

Whosoever shall call on the name of the Lord shall be saved.

-Acts 2:21b

Thou wilt keep him in perfect peace, whose mind is stayed on thee.

-Isaiah 26:3a

Discretion shall preserve thee,

understanding shall keep thee.

~Proverbs 2:11

Thou has been a shelter for me.

~Psalm 61:3a

Peace I leave with you,

my peace I give unto you

~John 14:27a

The peace of God shall keep your

hearts and minds.

~Philippians 4:7

The Lord is my shepherd;

I shall not want.

~Psalms 23:1

Honor the Lord with they

substance and with the first fruits

of all thine increase.

~Proverbs 3:9

For the Lord shall be thy confidence, and shall keep they foot from being taken.

~Proverbs 3:26

Blessed are the pure in heart; for

they shall see God.

~Matthew 5:8

If ye ask anything in my name,

I will do it.

~John 14:14

I will never leave thee,

nor forsake thee.

~Hebrews 13:5c

Blessed are they which do hunger

and thirst after righteousness;

for they shall be filled.

~Matthew 5:6

Draw nigh to God, and he will

draw nigh to you.

~James 4:8a

Blessed are the meek for they shall

inherit the earth.

~Matthew 5:5

My sheep hear my voice,

and I give them eternal life.

~John 10:27-28

He that dwelleth in the secret

place of the most high shall

abide under the shadow

of the Almighty.

~Psalm 91:1

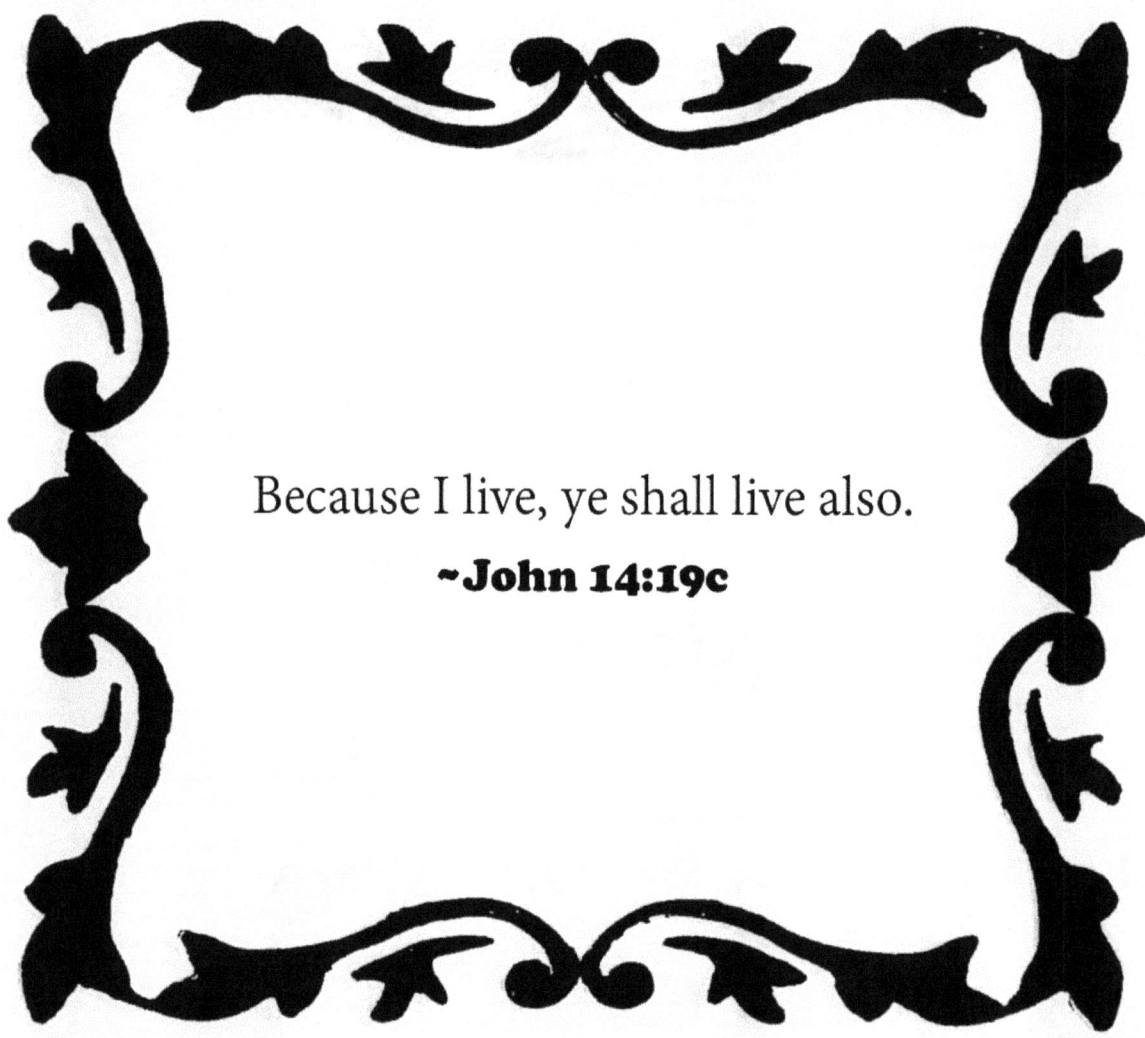

Because I live, ye shall live also.

~John 14:19c

In all thy ways acknowledge him,

and he shall direct thy paths.

~Proverbs 3:6

Come unto me, all ye that are

heavy laden,

and I will give you rest.

~Matthew 11:28

Humble yourselves in the sight of

the Lord, and he shall lift you up.

~James 4:10

The same Lord over all is rich

unto all that call upon him.

~Roman 10:12b

I will bless the Lord at all times;

his praise shall continually

be in my mouth.

~Psalm 34:1

He that humbles himself

shall be exalted.

~Matthew 23:12b

When a man's ways please the
Lord, he maketh even his enemies
to be a peace with him.

~Proverbs 16:7

I will not leave you comfortless.

~John 14:18a

A PRAYER TO REMEMBER

Thank you God for my caring and loving
parents. Thank you God for parents
who taught me to pray.
Amen.

"Remember, sometimes parents may seem old-fashioned and boring,
but their wisdom is priceless."

Why didn't somebody tell me
that next to choosing Christ
as my personal savior,
choosing my spouse would be
the most important decision of my life?

~Dr. Francesica Kelley

If you have been blessed or influenced
by the contents of this book,
I would love to hear from you.
Please contact me at:

Dr. Francesica Kelley
5022 Rixie Road
North Little Rock, AR 72217
(501) 412-9274

Email: kelleyenterprise2@gmail.com
Email: fran@positivepeoplepromotions.org

Website: www.positivepeoplepromotions.org

Note: A portion of the proceeds from the sale of this book will benefit the Positive People non-profit tutoring/mentoring program.

About the Author

"You are Blessed and Anointed"

A 23-year, 2-time breast cancer survivor, Author Francesica Kelley's passion has always been helping others. Dr. Kelley has been a Gospel Radio announcer for over 30 Years and is President Emeritus of the Arkansas Gospel Announcers Guild. She is a hard working woman who has a heart after God, those who can't do for themselves; her family and her community.

A devoted wife, mother, grandmother, and great-grandmother, Dr. Kelley is also a licensed ordained minister and active member of The St. Luke Baptist Church, Rev. Eric Alexander is pastor.

Founder and President of Positive People Promotions, Inc. organized in 1998, Dr. Kelley started this non-profit organization in order to empower students and improve life in the community.

The organization believes that in order to reach those goals, we must start early with our youth, giving them a strong foundation of diverse resources.

A Note From The Publisher

As a publisher, I am blessed to experience so much love from the authors who come to me for my assistance. Most books are healing, some are entertaining, and some inform. The thread that overwhelmingly and consistently binds us all together as a 'Butterfly Family' is the desire to assist, empower, and inspire.

Dr. Kelley is offering, in this one book, so much to so many. Yes, the targeted audience are the children, but I have no doubt that this book will also shed light for many adults as well. Life is so much easier when you know who you are, what you're purposed to do, and given basic instruction on how to move forward.

"Why Didn't Somebody Tell Me" is a book that addresses what most of us take for granted—manners and decency. In today's society, we seem to have lost our humanity!

No matter the reason, there is hope for restoration.

I will personally make sure that each of my grandchildren have a copy of Dr. Kelley's book and I applaud YOU for making the wise decision to offer it to the child(ren) in your life.

Congratulations to Dr. Kelley and welcome to the family, my *friend* Fran.

Love you to life,

~Iris M. Williams

Tops of The Trees Books

An imprint of Butterfly Typeface Publishing

WWW.BUTTERFLYTYPEFACE.COM

www.ingramcontent.com/pod-product-compliance
Lightning Source LLC
Chambersburg PA
CBHW080519090426
42734CB00015B/3109